—JOY—

Joy

Beautiful Writings
To Make Your Heart Sing

Selected by

Lois Huffmon Hunt

Illustrated by

Arlene Noel

Hallmark Editions

-ᎯᎾᏝ-

The sun does not shine
for a few trees and flowers,
but for the wide world's joy.

Henry Ward Beecher

The happy mood—
it's lovely, and it's mine,
and I shall not expose it
to the wind, the weather
or the world's comments;

in a green-edged corner

      of my heart I'll enclose it

with mist and moonbeams...

     and it needn't make sense!

            Florence Jacobs

When one has much
to put in them,
a day has a hundred pockets.

Friedrich Nietzsche

he world
was beautiful....
The moon and the stars
were beautiful,

the brook, the shore,
the forest and rock...
the flower and butterfly
were beautiful.

Hermann Hesse

The happiest moments
of my life have been
in the flow of affection
among friends.

Thomas Jefferson

A sorrow shared
is but half a trouble,
but a joy that's shared
is a joy made double.

Old Proverb

Happiness is a sunbeam
which may pass
through a thousand bosoms
without losing a particle
of its original ray.

Sir Philip Sidney

Each moment of the year
has its own beauty...
a picture
which was never seen before
and which
shall never be seen again.

Ralph Waldo Emerson

I remember running
over the hills just at dawn
one summer morning and,
pausing to rest in the silent woods,
saw, through an arch of trees,
the sun rise
over river, hill,

and wide green meadows
as I never saw it before.
Something born of the lovely hour,
a happy mood,
and the unfolding aspirations
of a child's soul
seemed to bring me
very near to God....

Louisa May Alcott

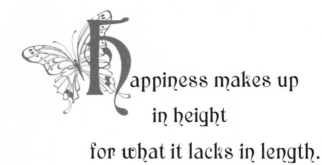

Happiness makes up
in height
for what it lacks in length.

Robert Frost

A year is...

the sparkle of snowflakes,

the sweet melody of robins,

the fragrance of roses,

and the gold and ruby

of fallen leaves.

A year is three hundred
sixty-five days of beauty…
Three hundred
sixty-five reasons
for joy.

Mary Dawson Hughes

To me, every hour
of the day and night
is an unspeakably
perfect miracle.

Walt Whitman

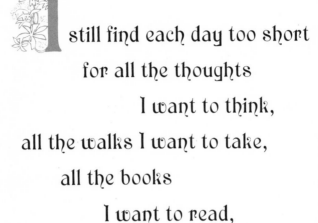

I still find each day too short
for all the thoughts
I want to think,
all the walks I want to take,
all the books
I want to read,

and all the friends I want to see.
The longer I live
the more my mind dwells
upon the beauty
and the wonder of the world.

John Burroughs

Happiness is a butterfly
which when pursued
is just beyond your grasp...
but if you will sit down quietly,
may alight upon you.

Nathaniel Hawthorne

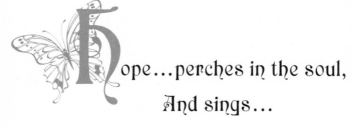

Hope…perches in the soul,

And sings…

And never stops at all.

Emily Dickinson

For me it is enough to say
That something beautiful
passed my way.

Ida Catherine Rohlf

Love is like a rose,
     the joy of all the earth....
Love is like a lovely rose,
     the world's delight.

Christina Rossetti

Joy sings in beauty
that surrounds us...
Joy smiles through loved ones
all around us...

JOY speaks in gentle words
that guide us…
JOY smiles in feelings
deep inside us.

Barbara Burrow

How beautiful
        a day can be
when kindness touches it.

George Elliston

The happiness of life
is made up of the little charities
of a kiss or smile,
a kind look,
a heartfelt compliment.

Samuel Taylor Coleridge

This world,

after all our science and sciences,

is still a miracle,

wonderful, inscrutable,

magical and more,

to whosoever will think of it.

Thomas Carlyle

The happiest people
seem to be those
who have no particular cause
for being happy
except the fact
that they are so....

Dean William Ralph Inge

Yesterday
is already a dream,
and tomorrow is only a vision;
but today, well=lived,

makes every yesterday
a dream of happiness,

and every tomorrow
a vision of hope.

from The Sanskrit

appy times
and bygone days
are never lost....
In truth, they grow
more wonderful
within the heart
that keeps them.

Kay Andrew

Hand set in Pacific at Hoflund-Schmidt
Typographic Services, Inc.
Printed on Hallmark Eggshell Book paper.
Designed by Rainer K. Koenig.